Fitness
Economics
For a Healthy Body and Mind

Ron Henderson

DEDICATION

This book is dedicated to my clients and friends who allowed me the pleasure of investing in their most valuable asset: their health.

CONTENTS

ACKNOWLEDGMENTS

First of all, I thank my Lord and Savior, Jesus Christ, who has given me, not only the gift of salvation and great health, but also the passion to lead others down the road to physical fitness.

A special thanks to my wife for her countless hours spent editing and her encouragement to see this book through to fruition.

Thanks to Lesly Keaton, for her friendship and initial work of editing this book.

Thanks to Steve Shapiro for his words of encouragement and willingness to help out in any way that he could.

Thanks to David Grossman of Grossman Design for his patience and cover design as well as his words of support and encouragement.

Thanks to my clients who allowed me to share their personal stories of transformation from physical bankruptcy to physical solvency and to those who believed enough in this book to give their personal endorsements.

INTRODUCTION

Money is the one thing that everyone can relate to—either you have it or you don't. We are taught the value of money early in life: those that have money can do things that those who don't have money can't. In my profession, I have had the opportunity to meet a wide array of people and I am always surprised to meet those who are at the top of their profession career wise but are at the bottom of the barrel where their health is concerned. By the time most people realize that they are physically bankrupt a lot of the damage is done. The good news is the bad news does not have to be permanent. With *Fitness Economics* I have utilized tried-and-true financial principles and developed them into physical health and fitness strategies to help individuals no matter what stage of life or fitness.

I know an individual who has been in and out of my life for over 14 years. He would start a fitness program and do well for a month or two then, because of work and his drive for corporate success, he would put his training program on hold. He picked up more accounts, made more deals, and accumulated more money. He would then come back to me, usually in worse shape than when he left, with good intentions to stay focused on his quest to become physically fit. At one point, he trained with me for six month straight, lost a significant amount of weight, and transformed his body. But, once again, the pursuit of making money or climbing the corporate ladder took him off of his commitment to good health. As much as he didn't want to admit it, his career had more priority in his life than his own health and fitness. Can I say for sure that money was the reason he stopped taking care of himself? No, but what I do know is that what we value we will protect and what we love the most will be at the top of our priority list.

The inspiration to write *Fitness Economics* came from the desire to create a system that would not only motivate an individual to want to change but would also provide easy to apply and easy to remember strategies to help those changes become a reality. I believe you will find the principles of fitness economics to be a catalyst to increase your health portfolio and keep you on the path to physical fitness and freedom.

PRIVACY

In this book, I have included stories of real men and women who have over-come many different challenges in their journey toward physical health and fitness. They have candidly shared their stories and, out of sensitivity to their privacy, some of their names may have been changed.

1 GETTING STARTED
If you can move you can improve!

Why Fitness Economics?

Everybody can relate to money. Whether it is investing, losing, saving, or spending, the dollar bill seems to have great influence in most people's lives. Those who have a lot of money approach life differently than those who are struggling to make ends meet. Even individuals who make a practice out of giving to those less fortunate are keenly aware of the benefits of having a balanced budget. *Fitness Economics* highlights the parallels between health and wealth. Just as planning and executing financial exchanges has become second nature to most people on a daily basis so can planning and executing a workable fitness program. *Fitness Economics* was designed to be a common sense approach to lifestyle fitness that motivates the reader to make the necessary changes to achieve their optimal health portfolio. Yes, you CAN achieve a balanced health budget. You CAN have energy to spare. You CAN plan for an active and vibrant retirement with enough vigor to achieve your dreams.

Economics 101

Economics is part of everyone's life whether you realize it or not. You deal with economics when you are planning what to make for dinner or when choosing the filling station with the lowest gas prices. You can't escape it. Even if you became a hermit living off by yourself you would still use economics as you decide how many vegetables to grow or rabbits to hunt to get you through the winter! For some, the term can make you roll your eyes or yawn. For others, you may roll up your sleeves and be eager to talk taxes, mergers, IRA's and the finer details of the stock market. Similar to how you think and use economics in everyday life, you can learn to habitually think and use fitness economics each day. My desire is that when anyone hears the term 'fitness economics', they get excited because they have mastered the art of living well physically.

Fitness Economics will help you understand your body's checks and balances, exchange physically depleting activities and habits for energizing actions, harness the motivation to be and stay fit, and offset physical challenges to achieve optimal health now and in the future. You will discover that a fit body is more efficient and better able to withstand stressors. With increased energy you are better able to meet the needs of yourself and others and improve mood and focus. *Fitness Economics* is not a quick fix for losing weight but a program for revitalizing your mind and body toward optimal fitness and longevity. Engage your heart and mind with *Fitness Economics* and let me take you on a journey toward improving your health portfolio.

Attitude

The best way to jump-start any program is by having the right attitude. But what exactly is attitude? Merriam-Webster defines it as "a position assumed for a specific purpose," "a mental position with regard to a fact or state," and "a feeling or emotion toward a fact or state." When we think of attitude we can put it in terms of one's mental disposition and bodily posture which expresses action. To make it more relevant to our discussion we can say that attitude is having a (strong) mental position and (strong) physical action. Becoming physically fit starts with mental determination or mental attitude that this is something you are going to accomplish.

It is very easy to say, "Okay, I'll now have a good attitude regarding..." Haven't we all tried from time to time to change our attitude about something and end up finding ourselves stuck with the same old attitude? Perhaps the mindset you attempted to change was about those annoying practices of a sibling when you were growing up or those ridiculous habits of a co-worker. Sometimes you may even have bad attitudes about yourself. Knowing that the right attitude or mental determination is required in order to reach a goal of any kind, how can we develop the appropriate attitude that will allow us to achieve victory in our most valuable asset: our health?

First, you must believe that you CAN change. If you don't believe it, it just won't happen. Make a commitment and be determined that you will keep it. Just doing this first thing will help you begin to believe in yourself. By making this first step of commitment you will prove to yourself that you can change. Any project is easier to accomplish for those who believe that they can. If you are having trouble believing you can change for life, try believing that you can change for one week. Picture yourself practicing your new attitude about health and fitness for seven short days and you will find that you CAN do it. You CAN change for the better. As a personal trainer I have noticed over the years that the people who believed they could change did so at a quicker pace. It's all about commitment and applied action.

Second, watch those thoughts that come to your mind. Start listening to what you are saying on the inside. You will no doubt hear yourself thinking negatively about your new commitment or coming up with excuses which get you out of meeting your goals. Replace those thoughts with thoughts that will bring about a positive attitude. For example, you may consciously or unconsciously think, "I have so much work to do today that I just don't have time to keep my exercise commitment." Replace that thought with, "I want to live a healthy life. I want to be around to enjoy the fruit of my labor." If you have children or grandchildren, replace "I'm too old and tired" with statements such as, "I want to have more energy to play with my grandchildren so I will keep my commitment to exercise." Learn to listen to and focus on your inner thoughts. When you catch yourself being negative by thinking or saying things that can defeat you, hit the "delete key" and insert the statements that reflect what you are ultimately looking for. I personally refuse to have a bad day or to return rudeness for rudeness. I refuse to lower myself to the base standards of some people I encounter but try to deposit positivity whenever I can. I didn't always think that way. I used to let almost anything affect my day but I had to decide to make the change. You are in charge of your attitude. Don't allow anyone, even yourself, to ruin your attitude.

Remember, your mental disposition is that of a positive or negative attitude. When it comes to becoming physically fit, that positive attitude is crucial to getting your body to respond with the appropriate physical action. Make the commitment, replace negative thoughts with positive thoughts, and keep the commitment. It is important that you realize your attitude has power over everything you do. For example, you may realize that something is right or good for you and make the necessary plans to achieve that 'rightness' in your life. You can get on your computer and map out all of the steps you need to accomplish the change. It looks good on paper and sounds good as you rehearse your mental flow chart, but to make it a reality you need to have the attitude that YOU CAN DO IT! Develop a strong mental attitude about becoming physically fit. Create a picture in your mind of how you want to look, feel, move, and live for the rest of your life. This means even into your senior years. We put considerable effort into securing our financial future, why don't we do the same for our future health and fitness? Now, take a glimpse of how you will likely look, feel, move, and live out your years without becoming physically fit. Do you want to look back on your life and say, "If only I had made proper deposits into my fitness account"? Taking the time to carefully and meaningfully focus on the fact that you can have some control on your future years right now can help you develop that strong mental attitude that will make you successful. Now is the time!

A successful business isn't built with an apathetic mindset. Well-groomed yards are not kept by accident. Retirement accounts are not built haphazardly but are built with a plan that has the later years in mind. How does anyone build a company? Or expand their businesses? Or purchase that new home? Or fund their children's college tuition? An old adage says that those who fail to plan, plan to fail. The same holds true when people don't set a plan in motion to take care of their health. Which one of the words below describes the mindset that you have had or seen others use to achieve financial success?

Adamant

Firm

Fixed

Obstinate

Persevering

Persistent

Purposeful

Relentless

Tenacious

Start thinking about what you want to change or improve and apply the action that is necessary to affect that change. Several weeks ago I ran into a friend of mine that used to value his health. He has since invested countless hours into his business and it is prospering. But sadly, when I saw him I did not recognize him. He looked like he was well into his late sixties but he was only fifty-five years old. The only thing increasing on him health wise was his belly. On one hand he is prospering but in the most important area of his life he was not. We all make choices on where we want to invest our time and energy and those choices are reflected in our attitudes and what we commit to.

You have the opportunity to increase your health net worth and to add to your health portfolio. When people see the need to change but don't it is like opening a bank account with $5,000 and then withdrawing $1,000 per day until the account is overdrawn. The bank would send you a notice stating that you are overdrawn. You get the notice but keep on writing checks without the funds to cover them. That is what so many people do. They write checks with their bodies that they can't afford to cash. They do that by ignoring the doctor's report, ignoring the television commercials, ignoring their family history, and so on, as though things will get better on their own. Well, they won't get better on their own. You must deposit daily into your health bank account if you want to reap great rewards.

Values

A friend of mine has at least five cars and most of them are collector cars which he drives only occasionally. I have wondered for years why he was so infatuated with cars. Is it the size of the engine? Is it the speed? Is it the sleek lines or the massive frames? For so many people, they care more about what they drive than the body they walk around in. It is not unusual for a person to put a lot of time and research into buying a car. They want to k now they can trust the person they are buying from and the mechanic who will maintain the care. They are fussy about the brand of gasoline or the type of oil they use. They check the car's oil and tire pressure regularly and make sure it gets scheduled maintenance. So why does their physical well-being not get the same attention? After all, is it not their most important asset?

This must change if a person wants to live a long and prosperous life. Your body has the ability to move you around for years. You can go fast or you can go slowly; you can be massive or you can be sleek. It all depends on how well you take care of yourself. When I was young I used to enjoying watching the TV show 'Knight Rider' with the car that was able to talk. Well, our bodies are talking to us every day but are we listening? People wake up in the morning and their dehydrated bodies are screaming for water but they grab coffee instead. They leave work feeling drained and then they slump their bodies down on their couches while, all along, their bodies are crying out, "Exercise! Exercise! More Exercise!" Exercise to your body is like oil to your car: if you don't keep oil in your car you will burn out the engine and if you don't exercise you will eventually run down your body.

There is nothing wrong with having material things, but when the things we have become more important than the individual that purchased them, then this is an issue. I have watched people for years get into the rut of trying to obtain more money, more merchandise, more property, and more of everything else. Most have developed the 'keeping up with the Jones' attitude. But what price are you willing to pay for good health? I hope your answer is anything and everything. If it is, my friend, then make a decision to change your future right now. Without this paradigm shift you will be heading down a road that will receive you with open arms but a road that is burdened with low energy, health problems, and a poor quality of physical life. As long as we are living we have a choice to affect the quality of our physical lives. Ask yourself, "What do I want my quality of life to be like?"

Ready to Begin

Now that you are ready to take the journey to physical health and fitness, take a moment to complete the 'Beginning Self-Encouragement Questionnaire'. This is a self-assessment tool to help you define your goals and acknowledge any attitudes that are contrary to meeting those goals. Remember, YOU CAN DO THIS!

BEGINNING SELF-ENCOURAGEMENT
QUESTIONNAIRE

1. Do you want to improve your physical health and fitness? If your answer was yes, list the reasons below in the order of their importance. If your answer was no, look for your receipt and return this book for your money back, because no amount of encouragement will help those that don't desire to change.

    a._____

    _____

    b._____

    _____

    c._____

    _____

    d._____

    _____

2. What do you feel exercise will do for you?

    _____

    _____

    _____

    _____

3. When do you plan to take the actions necessary to affect this change?

_____

4. Where do you see yourself being health-wise three months from now?

_____

_____

_____

Six months _____

_____

_____

One year_____

_____

_____

5. What detrimental attitudes have kept you from moving forward with commitment to a fitness program?

_____

_____

_____

_____

Remember, YOU have the power to change. Determine to turn any bad attitudes into positive ones and keep your eyes on your fitness goals. You can do it! After filling out this questionnaire read it back to yourself at least seven times. This will help to reinforce your conscience and help you take the appropriate action to obtaining your goals. Bookmark all the self-assessment pages in *Fitness Economics* and revisit them as you continue on your journey toward health and fitness.

2 GETTING STARTED
If health is wealth then why aren't we healthier?

If you don't know where you are, you can't plan the strategy to get to where you want to be. This is the point where you need to be honest with yourself. It may not be pleasant to face the physical and mental realities of where you are right now but it is essential to keep moving forward. Just like knowing your credit score, knowing your 'health score' will give you a fixed starting point by which you can gauge your progress in three areas: physiological, physical endurance, and mental/emotional stamina. Your health score will also reveal how vigorously you should progress and what medical steps you may need to take. As with any fitness program, it is important get the go-ahead from your doctor.

Mirror Yourself

If you have ever taken any type of sales training course then you have probably heard the term 'mirroring'. It is a common sale technique used to make the buyer feel more comfortable. What the sales person does is try to mirror the prospective buyer. If the buyer leans forward when they're talking, so does the sales person. If the buyer talks at a little slower pace, so does the sales person. Whatever the prospective buyer does the sales person tries to duplicate. The idea is that this 'mirroring' will make the prospective buyer feel more comfortable because of the commonality between the two.

When I speak of mirroring, I mean mirroring yourself. When using this technique it causes the user to feel a little uncomfortable. Why? Because you are taking the time to constructively evaluate yourself and, for some, this will be extremely uncomfortable. When you're ready to address the mirror, strip down and take a good look at yourself. Do you like what you see? If you do, then that is great and you need to ask yourself what you need to do to keep that youthful physique as you age. If you don't like what you see then what are you going to do about it? Do you love yourself enough to take care of what is before you? What we don't value, we don't love. Think about it. Have you ever had a girlfriend, a wife, a husband, or even a pet that you really loved? You showered them with gifts, the best food, flowers (well, maybe not for the pet), treats, and so on because you cared. But do you treat your body like you truly love yourself? If people did, their bodies would reflect that love in how it looks and feels. Maybe your stomach sticks out more than your chest, maybe your breasts are saggy, maybe you get tired easily; whatever it is, you can do something to help improve the quality of your physical life.

If you are physically fit then recession can hit you tomorrow and you could say, "No problem!" If the government cut your social security you could say, "We knew they would cut it eventually, but I am ready. I've got my energy and my health." If they increase your taxes tomorrow it probably won't feel good, but none of those things will have any bearing on where you are health-wise, unless you allow it. My friend, it does not take a lot of space to do push-ups and you can walk anywhere. Parks are plentiful. In an unstable economy you can be feeling good physically and mentally. That's right—mentally—because an active body helps the mind as well.

PHYSIOLOGICAL HEALTH SCORE

It is common knowledge that being physically fit decreases your risk of acquiring many health issues. In addition, getting physically fit will greatly improve many existing health conditions. Diabetes, heart disease, esophageal reflux, some cancers, arthritis, and many other diseases may be prevented or improved by getting your eating and exercise on track. That's good news! You can live longer and healthier by taking care of your most valuable asset.

Your physiological health score will give you an idea of how your body processes are functioning. Measurements such as blood pressure, heart rate, cholesterol, HDL, LDL, and others let you know how well you are taking care of your body and if you are having primary health issues. They also provide a starting point by which you can gauge your progress. Your doctor will recommend a set of tests that are appropriate for you. Generally, you can count on the ones listed above, as well as hemoglobin and a set of electrolytes. If you are age fifty or older, you may be encouraged to have a colon screening for cancer. Prostate checks, mammograms, and pap smears are also a part of preventative health care.

From Flab to Fit

In 1984 I was training a man who was considered obese by his doctor. This bachelor had a hugely successful business but was failing in almost every area of his health. He smoked, drank, and did not exercise. Like a lot of individuals, his job became his life. He confided in me that his being single had a lot to do with how he felt about himself and how he looked. After about four months of intense training three days a week this man began sporting a V-shaped physique. His physical improvement increased his self-confidence and prompted him to invest in other areas of his life. With a new haircut and a new attitude, this single man now had four women vying for his affection. This happened all because he decided to increase his health portfolio to the level of his financial portfolio. When he first came to me he could have anything that money could buy, but he lacked something that money can't buy and that was great health. A trainer can help you achieve great results, but he/she can't force you to train; that is on you.

New Lease on Life

Many years ago, an older gentleman who owned one of the biggest law firms in Minnesota knocked on my office door. I had been told that he might come by to talk about the possibility of training. Within minutes of our talk he told me that he had a small heart attack and needed to get in better shape. The man's countenance was that of someone in their middle sixties, but his movement was of someone closer to eighty. His gait was very slow as though he was using a walker. After training this man for about one year he developed a physique of someone who probably played college ball. He moved so fast that I would occasionally ask him to slow down a bit, and, instead of looking and moving like an aged senior citizen, he looked at least 10 years younger than his actual age! This man now moves with vigor and was ready to take up self-defense lessons. I am giving you this insight so you will understand that no one but you can hold you back. Great health is one decision away...do it today. If you say you don't like exercise, well, that's alright. You probably did not like having to knuckle down and save for your kids' college fund either but you did because it was the right and the smart thing to do. Taking care of YOU is the smartest thing you will ever do.

PHYSICAL ENDURANCE SCORE

Your physical endurance score is a measure of your overall endurance relative to your natural physical make-up. There are many different body types and each has its strengths and weaknesses. For example, take a look at champion marathon runners. They are toned, sleek, and have amazing legs and long-distance lung power. Then observe professional weight lifters. Could you imagine those solid, stocky athletes running a marathon? Now that might be fun to watch! Gymnasts are flexible and petite while football players are usually large with ample muscle mass. These athletes made the most of their natural make-up.

Let's go back to the mirror: What are your natural attributes? What is your potential? Imagine what you would look like if you invested in fine-tuning those natural attributes. Imagine how strong arms, strong legs, and toned abdominal muscles would feel. Think about what a regular investment of exercise and muscle training would do for you. Maybe winning a marathon is not in your future but imagine the feeling of strength as you climb those five flights of stairs to your office with ease. Make a mental picture of yourself walking, moving, and playing in your potential. Keep that picture readily available and look at it often. It will help you stay motivated.

Strength to Give

A good friend and client of mine recently found herself caring for her husband who was having serious joint problems. After months of trying to deal with the problem, he checked into the Mayo Clinic. Several weeks later he was in a heavy cast that covered his lower body. The reason for sharing this story is that my friend is in her mid-sixties and now has the unexpected job of taking care of her beloved husband. She has to change him, bathe him, and push him up a ramp in a wheelchair. Consequently, with all this time being spent on her husband, she had not worked out with me in almost seven weeks. When I asked her if she had time to do any exercise at home, she plainly stated that, yes, lifting and pushing and pulling her husband around *was* her exercise! She said that these are all the things she couldn't have done if she had not spent the time investing into her health all these years.

Before she started training with me my friend couldn't even do two push-ups on her knees. Because she took the time to make those little deposits into her health account, a year later she was able to do thirty regular push-ups. That is why she now has the physical strength to take care of her husband. I would hate to imagine her situation if she had not invested into her health. This all started by my friend looking at herself in the mirror and, not placing judgment on herself, but honestly accessing her physical situation much the way we do when we are in a financial crisis. We do an evaluation and see where can we cut back and make adjustments. Well, it is time to do that evaluation. There is still time. If you are reading this then it is not too late to take action.

Sophia's Story

Sofia is a lady that hates exercise but does it because she knows that it's the prudent thing to do. She has three lovely daughters and wants to be around to see them enjoy life, see them have kids, and enjoy being a grandmother. To ensure that she has the strength to embrace all her life has to offer she exercises on a regular basis. She can proudly say that, because of her investments in her physical fitness, she was able to install five sets of home windows by herself and still had energy left to enjoy her family. Her investments have also paid off in giving her more energy and a younger look. When she first came to me she was physically bankrupt and now she has the look of physical solvency. She is energetic and full of life. She did what she did not want to do to get what she knew she needed.

I personally have never liked paying for new tires but I could not imagine driving around in Minnesota winters with bad tires. I also don't like paying for car insurance but I pay for it so I can legally drive. In fact, most people would say you are a fool if you can afford car insurance and don't have it. Why would anyone wait for a crisis? It's time to treat your body with the same consideration. Become intentional and start exercising.

Strength and Confidence

In 1992, a tall and scrawny man who I'll call 'Mike' came to my office seeking my services. Mike, admittedly, was not a confident man. When I asked him what he wanted to improve health-wise, he replied that he wanted to really improve his overall physique with a bigger chest, bigger arms, broader back, increase his leg strength, and gain some weight. In less than a year of training, Mike had become confident and looked more like a professional wrestler who was in shape than the '98 pound weakling' that first approached me. What was it that made Mike want to take the steps towards change and then stick with it? Well, in his own words, he said he was "...sick and tired of feeling bad about myself and sick and tired of not having any energy." He got to the place of being ready to commit. I ended up training Mike for almost three years. He still looks good to this day.

MENTAL/EMOTIONAL STAMINA SCORE

Mental and emotional stamina score relates your ability to process information with clarity and to experience consistent emotional balance. Are you forgetful and easily distracted? Does it seem like you just don't think as quickly on your feet as you used to? How about your emotions? Are you easily stressed? Do you find yourself being more irritable as the day goes on? It has long been held that exercise causes your brain to release the 'feel good' substance known as endorphins. You may have even heard the term 'runner's high.' Not only does exercise give you a sense of well-being but research shows that up to 24 hours after aerobic exercise it is easier for the brain to grow new neurons and neural connections. Exercise also may delay dementia, reduce effects of brain damage from Alzheimer's disease, and keep you thinking young. Exercise is the gift that keeps on giving! On the diet side, we all know what too much caffeine, sugar, and alcohol can do to a person's mind and emotions. The culminating balance of neglecting both exercise and a healthy diet is a deficit of self-confidence, sluggishness, discouragement, stress, and frustration. A consistent investment in diet and exercise reaps a huge return for your mind and emotions.

Ellen's Story

Several years ago a man came to me for my personal training services and after about four months he asked me to train his wife as well. He said he thought that weight training and exercise would be very good for her. I asked him what kind of shape she was in and he said she was slim but needed to tone up. More importantly, he felt exercise would help her state of mind. See, several years ago Ellen had attempted suicide and her husband thought that exercise training, along with my positive attitude and outlook on life, would be great for her...if she would show up! At that time in her life Ellen found it very hard to commit to anything. Well, she did show up! And this is her story—short, honest, and to the point:

> I used to sleep all the time because I really didn't know how to deal with life and a lot of the things that were going on in my mind. Sleep was like the drug that kept me safe and away from the chaos of life. Because of my manic-depressive personality I felt like I was one big mess. My head was racing around! I was unstable and mentally imbalanced. This really did not calm down until I started exercising consistently. I not only felt better but it calmed my mind and my mood. Because I was on a structured training program it also seemed to mellow out the dragon that seemed to be roaring inside of me. After several months of exercising, my husband noticed that I was calmer and my children even noticed. I still am somewhat manic, but, as they used to say in those old commercials, "I've come along way, baby!" Yes, from the chaotic to the committed, from not being able to stand in one place for more than a few minutes to exercising three

days a week, I am now making regular deposits into my health bank account. And, although I stopped for a while, I am back at it—back to training with the Fitness King! Back to making the only deposits that really count in life.

Ellen's decision to invest in her health bank account has helped her physically *and* mentally as well as gave her a more positive outlook.

Grief

Over my many years as a personal trainer, I have encountered numerous people who have had to go through the heart-wrenching experience of losing a loved one. It can be trying on your body, mind, and emotions. There is no way to take away all the pain or to limit grief to an event instead of a process, but taking care of your body's need for movement can help you better handle these difficult times.

One of my clients, Andrea, had first-hand experience in dealing with grief after the loss of her beloved husband. She found that tending to her physical fitness program helped her get through the grieving process with more resilience. She writes:

> Physical fitness has played such an important role in my life, especially during my recent time of grieving. It allowed my body and mind the ability to cope. It was the catalyst that moved me forward; that kept me on the healing track and gave me the strength to adapt to new changes and challenges. Effective coping tips for grieving are as different and as numerous as there are grieving individuals. Caring for oneself through physical activity, continuing nutritious and regular eating habits, and getting extra rest are keys to ease the grief

process. Unfortunately, people usually handle stress while sitting at their desk or in their cars stuck in traffic. Exercise, on the other hand, helps to avoid the damage to our health that prolonged stress can cause.

Andrea is an example of how exercise, rest, and proper nutrition can help gird you up during particularly stressful times. You can't avoid sorrow in this life, but you can be better prepared to handle it when it comes your way.

Keeping Chaos at Bay

I have been fortunate enough to have good friends in my life. In 1975 I had the great pleasure to become good friends with a man I will call Steve. When I met Steve he was working out like there was no tomorrow. He was a former marine and I believe the consistency of that life style got him into the habit of running, lifting weights, and so on. Steve was one of these good natured types who are always in a good mood. He rarely ever seemed to be down. One day he was driving his car and was struck by an oncoming vehicle. He was hospitalized for weeks. Because of the bruising on his stomach and shoulders he was told that he should not exercise so he obeyed the doctor's orders. In fact, he did not workout consistently ever again. That accident got him out of the habit that used to be instinct. Because he was no longer exercising, issues like depression and bipolar disorder, which had been held at bay, was now at the forefront of his life. Now he is frequently down and depressed with anger issues. When I would suggest that he should start exercising again he would say, "I know you're right, brother," but he wouldn't do anything. My friend Steve is a classic example of how much exercise can help a person mentally. Within a two year period of his accident he had over two incidents of road rage and other physical altercations. I believe that if he would have kept exercising he would not have had many of those negative experiences in his life.

Maybe you are feeling a little down right now. Exercise can help you relieve a lot of stress and help you to feel better about yourself. When you feel a little down go to God and ask him to give you the strength to take the action that is necessary to change your life. Prayer works. I do it daily but it will take action to keep your body moving. So how about today? Are you ready to get your health back; to get your life back? If you are ready then simply start where you are right now. It's easier than you think. It is no different than a child taking that first step. You just have to take it!

There is nothing to it, but to do it!

MY HEALTH SCORE

Your health score is an indicator of areas you need to work on to improve your health portfolio. It is designed as a tool to help you in your pursuit and to alert you to any troubled areas that need extra focus. This is NOT a medical diagnostic tool and does not take the place of regular check-ups and screenings by a health care professional and their recommendations. Fill in your current readings and compare with the recommended 'normal' values. Commit to a program of diet, aerobic exercise, and fitness training. After three months come back and fill in your new readings and be encouraged by the results!

PHYSIOLOGICAL SCORE

Fill in your latest test results. If you have not had the readings done within the past year, we recommend consulting with your physician for recommendations.

Date: _____   Normal Readings   Date: _____

Weight _____   _____

BMI _____   18.5-24.9*   _____

(BMI-Body Mass Indicator calculation tool used is from Mayo Clinic at www.mayoclinic.com)
*BMI calculation may be higher for people who are very muscular and physically fit.

Blood
Pressure _____   Below 120/80   _____

Cholesterol _____   Below 200   _____

HDL _____   60 and above   _____

LDL _____   Below 100   _____

Triglycerides _____   Below 150   _____

PHYSICAL ENDURANCE

Physical endurance varies from person to person. What is normal endurance for one person may be far less or far more than another. Track your progress by recording your current physical ability, your ability after three months of applying Fitness Economics principles, and after six months.

1. How many steps can you walk up without getting winded?

Now_____   3 Months_____   6 Months _____

2. How many sit ups can you do?

Now_____   3 Months_____   6 Months_____

MENTAL/EMOTIONAL STAMINA SCORE

The mental and emotional stamina scoring is more subjective than the above sections. Only you can determine your mental and emotional satisfaction. For your own reflection, jot down how you are feeling now and then revisit this section after three months of applying Fitness Economics and again after six months. You will be pleased to see your progress.

NOW: On (date) ___/___/_____ my prevailing mood is _____. I (circle one) am or am not satisfied with this. My mental and emotional goal is _____

_____

_____

_____

3 MONTHS: After making the necessary changes in my life, my prevailing mood is _____. The changes I have seen in my mental and emotional stamina are _____.

6 MONTHS: After making the necessary changes in my life, my prevailing mood is _____. The changes I have seen in my mental and emotional stamina are _____

_____

_____

_____

Remember, the scoring above is designed to motivate you to take a 'look in the mirror' at your over-all health and to take the necessary steps toward physical responsibility. Only YOU can make those changes...and I know that YOU can do it! Pay yourself first by taking the time to assess and invest.

3 PAY YOUR SELF FIRST
There's nothing to it but to do it

Health: Our #1 Commodity

Your number one commodity is your health. It is one commodity that none of us should ever want to trade, yet most of us do so daily through neglect and over indulgence. People over-eat and over-strive for material success while neglecting their most valuable commodity. The desire to achieve has caused a lot of people to throw themselves out with the bath water so to speak. Like a failing business that is a lot harder to restore, it will take time and effort to get your body fit. Wouldn't it be nice if your body was like your computer and if you mess it up all you have to do is hit the restore button and you are back in business? Your body wasn't designed that way. If you stop exercising or fail to even start, atrophy starts to its own process, leaving your highly valued commodity at a low point. If you let your health and fitness cease to be a priority it will be much harder to restore what was lost.

Years of abuse and neglect may never be completely reversed but our bodies are incredibly forgiving if we take the time to be more bullish towards our physical assets and more aware of protecting our health. I have a friend who is really into the stock market. He constantly looks at where the stock is and what direction it is heading. When it looks like the stock is changing, whether up or down, he then makes a decision to trade or purchase more stock. Notice that I said he is *constantly* monitoring his stocks. Imagine if you took even a tenth of your time and monitored your health and then took action to increase or decrease what you are doing based on what you need and are receiving. When people start an exercise program they have the tendency to do too much too soon. In others words, people overly invest into their health as though they have the ability to drastically change themselves overnight. Because they did not take the time to analyze their health portfolio they were overly aggressive in their investment strategy and got injured. What kind of investment strategy are you planning and who is your investment advisor? Hopefully after reading this book you will be more motivated to monitor your health and take sensible and well advised action to improve.

Are You Physically Bankrupt?

You have heard of being financially bankrupt. It's happening to so many people these days. You can become physically bankrupt, as well, by continually neglecting your health bank account. One of my clients began training with me a few years ago. Upon arrival she was physically broke and near bankruptcy, weighing in at 320+ pounds at about 5'6". Breathing was difficult as she bent over to tie her shoes. After a year of weight training three times per week plus walking on her own two to three times a week, she lost 100 pounds. She has developed vigor, energy, and smiles much more frequently as she continues to remain physically fit over the years. She practices moderation in all areas of her life and has won the battle for physical independence. Just how did she do this? She had an attitude of determination, took the action to make things happen through physical fitness, and ate in moderation.

The way we eat has a significant impact on our health and physical fitness. The way we utilize money has a very significant impact on our overall financial stability. Take a look at this interesting comparison between food and finances:

FOOD	MONEY
What we make it to be	What we allow it to be
A necessity	For most a necessity
For some a way of life	For some it *is* their life
For some it is a reward	For some it is power
Many are addicted	Many are addicted
Some use it as an escape	Some find it to be freedom

WHAT SAY YOU? WHAT REPRESENTS YOU? WHERE DO YOU NEED TO CHANGE AND TAKE CHARGE?

Action Plan

So, you are reading this book. That means you have some interest and desire to make a change, right? Let me help you. You can do this! You want to become physically fit or maintain what has been accomplished. Let's look at the steps above and apply them to becoming physically fit. And in the meantime remember: You Can Do This!

1. **Pay yourself first physically.** Why? Because you value yourself! You would not be reading this book if you didn't. How do you pay yourself first physically? In the financial world you are told to save at least 10% of your monthly income. You pay your financial obligations to everyone else but it is just as important to pay yourself with the same diligence. In actuality, you value yourself more than your creditors, right? It is much more important to focus a percentage of your time on training your body first. What do I mean by first? It has to be at that level of priority. Even before you financially pay yourself that 10% of your monthly income, diligently make your daily physical payments to yourself.

2. **Make smart physical investments**. Why? Because you value your future! How many investments are out there for you to make? Countless! Walk, run, swim, lift weights, play sports, etc. Most importantly, have a fitness trainer so that you are making the right investments (it is somewhat like having a financial investor). An excellent trainer will focus on what you need to do with all the aspects of your body, how you should do it, how often, and what you need to change for the ultimate results. The trainer will keep you motivated for success and celebrate with you when you achieve those successes. Yes, you must INVEST in yourself for great health, as you would when INVESTING in your finances. Again, they are both important. It's very difficult to enjoy the wealth when the health has departed!

3. **Make automatic direct deposits**. When we use this method of paying bills it's easier. The money is "out of sight, out of mind." Whatever method you use to invest in your physical wellness, make it an automatic payment. Not only will the deposits be

automatic, you will be more likely to follow through on completing your investment in your physical health! Automated extras can be simple, everyday activities such as:

- Taking the stairs instead of the elevator.

- Washing dishes or your car by hand.

- Dancing to lively music while doing household chores.

- Using a push lawn mower instead of riding mower.

- Gardening

- Walking instead of riding whenever possible.

- Parking at the far end of the parking lot and walking to your destination.

- Eating a piece of fruit when you have a sweet craving instead of candy, pastry or other high carb, high fat treats.

- If you know how many breaks you get in your typical days' work, use the break time to eat your lunch and use your lunch time, which is usually longer, to take your 30 to 45 minute walk.

- Keep your bathroom newspaper and magazine free. Let's face it, where there is paper there is more time spent that you can be using to increase your health score.

- Use a shopping basket instead of a cart to haul

those few groceries you have; your biceps will thank for it.

- Use commercial breaks as the time to do a few push-ups or some jumping jacks. A great resource to help keep you on track is my set of Power Cards which were designed to be used during commercial breaks and comes with a structured program. Check out my website at www.fitnessking.com for more information about Power Cards and other fitness topics.

- Stand when you can, unless of course you have a job where you are standing all day, then you might want to sit with a lift—stomach in and chest held high.

- Shovel and rake by hand when you can: Fill your shovel with small loads as this won't put a strain on your back but will take you longer. When raking, make sure to switch directions; lead with one hand half the time and then the opposite hand the other.

There are many more automatic calorie-burning, energy-boosting automated extra's that you can deposit in your health bank account. Have fun! Start looking for creative ways to add your own throughout the day. You will be surprised and pleased in the long term.

4. **Make a physical fitness commitment and stick to it!** People do not reach their financial goals and dreams by making a January commitment and breaking it by March every year. (That will sound familiar if you've experienced this routine with your fitness plans of the past.) They would think it absurd to follow such logic and have a positive return. Since

YOU are serious about making a change, you now realize just how absurd it is to do this with your health.

5. **Make a decision—right now**. Write it down. Put today's date on it. Write down, a. what you are going to do, such as...work out three times/week for the next twelve months (better yet, for life!), b. when you are going to start, c. what needs to be done to get started such as getting a physical, finding a qualified fitness trainer, etc.

I'm passionate about having things in the correct priority. Pay YOUSELF first physically. I really want you to get this. You can own and then stack $1,000 bills as tall as the Statue of Liberty but that money will not be enjoyed by you if you don't have the necessary physical well-being. Money has not been able to cure the things that are killing people every day.

What is $500,000 minus $300,000?
Answer: $200,000

What's $500,000 minus health?
Answer: Zero, Nada, Nothing

The least we can do is value ourselves enough to take care of these precious bodies with which we've been entrusted. Some say that every day above ground is a good day. I say every day we increase our health dividends is a great day!

Team Up

Many people who begin an exercise program or who are ramping up their current regime find a workout partner to be beneficial as an encouragement and support. Not only can they provide camaraderie during your exercise but they can also be a reminder of your health commitment. Do you have a friend, a spouse, or a co-worker that would like to join you in your quest? If so, use this to your advantage! Someone who desires to live a long and healthy life (as you do!), and someone with whom you can be accountable as well as keep each other encouraged, can make a world of difference in keeping you on track. Be determined together to succeed in becoming and staying physically fit and don't allow yourself or each other to be distracted by other people or issues that can arise. Together be alert for things that will try to interfere in your joint quest to become physically fit.

Putting your hearts into the commitment you are making and keeping each other under accountability can greatly increase your success. This has a marvelous impact on the achievement of your goals because you are motivating each other. When one is not 'feeling it' today, the other is there to keep the momentum going. That level of consistency forms power and positive habits that can be utilized for life. This, of course, is your goal! So, if at all possible, get your spouse or friend involved to work together on having a new life of fitness, ensuring each other has the potential to live life to its fullest!

Pace

If someone put your favorite dessert in front of you—let's say chocolate cake—you would probably enjoy eating a piece (or maybe even two!) without hesitation. Yet, if you were asked to eat one or two entire cakes in one sitting that would be another story. Your initial excitement of consuming what is your favorite dessert would turn into a nightmare that could result in you feeling sick and never wanting to eat chocolate cake again. Your favorite would turn into your least favorite. Keep this analogy in mind when you begin your fitness program. You must consume small portions at a time.

When you began saving money, depending on the age and circumstances, it may have been difficult. By putting away a little at a time, over time, the positive habits developed as you watched your money grow and the interest earnings increased. Regular small deposits then became regular larger deposits. That financial discipline results in the attainment of goals, dreams, aspirations, or simply a nest egg in life.

As you begin your quest for physical fitness, apply the discipline that is needed to be successful by making small deposits in your health account. Small but regular consistent deposits with gradual increases will pay off in the long run. Your body deserves to have new habits introduced in a way that it won't be overwhelmed, either physically or emotionally. Doing too much at one time would be like devouring those two chocolate cakes! Set out to succeed by gently introducing the new behaviors so your body does not get overly exerted and your mind does not become convinced that your goals are unattainable. Don't sabotage your success!

Start out with the right amount of deposits for where you are physically right now. The best way to make that determination is to see your doctor before you start your exercise program. If your doctor gives you the go-ahead, then let your body and common sense become your guide. YOU CAN DO THIS! You are worth every deposit into your health account and more. You will thank yourself as you continue for the rest of your life. Yes, you are worth developing the strong attitude and mind so you can have the strong and healthy body that will help you live out your dreams. After all, what is the use of having dreams if you are not healthy enough to enjoy them? Deposit now and you will reap for many years to come.

Hedging Your Bet Physically

In our ever-changing world where one day things seem to look promising and the next day they are volatile, hedging your bet physically is a great plan. This is especially important today when health care issues are up in the air. No one is guaranteed that health care will be around when they need it or what health insurance will even cover. With more people working into their later years, hedging your bet is not only a wise decision but one that will increase your chances of a healthier and longer life. It may also save you thousands of dollars in health care cost and lost time away from work and family. The more that we do to better our health, the more our health portfolio will increase. Billions of dollars are being deposited into retirement accounts each year by those who thought it prudent to invest financially into their later years of life but how much is being deposited into their health bank accounts? People who learned to invest and save their money are not stressed over money issues because they have it. Similarly, those that have invested into their health have an improved quality of life. This improved quality of life will also lessen the pressure on their children because they are less likely to need physical assistance in their 'golden years'.

Life Assurance Plan

Do you have a life assurance plan? Not life insurance—life *assurance*. Have you thought about your future and where you want to be health wise? Are you prepared? Do you have a plan that will guarantee you better physical and mental health? If you don't, you are not alone. Millions of Americans have worked all their lives saving money for their retirement only to find themselves laid up in a respite home somewhere, all because they didn't prepare for their later life. To truly prepare for your later years, you must start now to develop and then maintain a consistent exercise program. When you prepare for your later years by eating healthier and exercising, you increase your chances of having a healthy rewarding life. I am not saying that you will be free from some physical challenges or health issues, but by keeping your body in the best shape possible, you will be positioning yourself to be much better physically prepared to handle the stress of any traumas much earlier. I have many friends well into their seventies that have the energy of someone forty—all because they took the time to invest into their health early in life. Don't have a life assurance plan? Why not? What is stopping you? This book is about helping people wake up and realize they can either make their lives easier or harder. Even if a disability has you in a wheelchair, you could reap increased benefits of a healthier lifestyle by exercising what you can and eating smaller meals.

Just like assessing what type of insurance policy fits your life and goals best, assess what lifestyle changes will be most beneficial for you. Ask yourself these questions: Does it meet your needs and your wants? What is it you really desire? What assistance will you need to accomplish your goals? Success is right around the corner if you are willing to pursue it. Unlike many insurance plans, fitness is affordable. It can cost you literally nothing if your regime is walking, biking, hiking, swimming, etc. It's practical because you start where you are and you do what you can. Your policy limits are self-set since how long you exercise is up to you. There is no age limit because exercise is an equal opportunity employer. Anyone can do it! If you can move, you can improve! Exercise is recession proof. It's an 'open 24-hour' business. Lastly, it pays high dividends which are realized in an increase in muscle strength and your ability to move better and with more freedom. It can slow down the aging process and let you move easier longer.

Life Lasting Social Security Plan

What is a social security plan? Well, a social security plan is your social network, which is your friends, your family, and really anyone who is willing to hold you accountable in sticking to your predetermined exercise plan. I have always believed in a person being consistent. In regards to exercise, as we get older and busier it is harder to maintain our course. It is essential to success to have a routine down. You may add or take away from this routine from time to time but the bulk of this routine will stay the same.

Active Example:

1. 30 minutes walking every day—this is a must whether you walk fast or slow.

2. Stretch for 5 to 10 minutes a day. This will help to keep you limber and less likely to injure yourself from small movements.

3. Active Extras three to four times weekly. For some it might be golfing, biking, or bowling. For others it might be swimming, tennis, or hiking. Mix and match but have FUN!

Invest Now or Pay Later

By investing into your health early on you are increasing your chance of having a long and rewarding life. None of us know when our time is up but what I do know is exercise will make you feel great and may enhance your appearance, as well as improve your self-confidence. Take the opportunity to pursue great health as someone would pursue an Olympic team. I have been watching the televised Olympic Games and it is fascinating to see the athletes' commitment to their sport. They live, eat, and sleep their sport, not only thinking about the present but also the future. Pursue great health like it is your last opportunity because this, in fact, may be the only time that you even feel motivated to start an exercise program. If you are feeling a tug towards exercise right now, take advantage of this and just start where you are. Don't worry about what your neighbor is doing or not doing—just keep yourself in the game and do what you know should be doing.

As I watched those Olympians receive their medals, I could not help but think of all the time and money invested into their sport and into their health. The Olympics is not the venue for unhealthy people but for those who are willing to go the extra mile, the extra day, and the extra months to perfect their sport and themselves physically. Each athlete trains in the present as he/she envisions his/her future to be an Olympic athlete. It takes dedication, commitment, and a great support system. As you start on your quest for great health, you too will have to train today with your future in mind. Whatever you want for your later years in life, train for it now and, as the years start to accumulate, you will be glad you invested early on.

At the ripe, young age of 58, I am one of the few adults in my community that actually climbs, runs, and jumps with their kids—all because I made exercise a priority. I am glad I made that choice. I also have many friends who look eight to twelve years younger than their age because they, too, made the decision to exercise consistently. Even people who have come to me who had never worked out before were able to add years to their life by exercising and eating healthier. I say this not to brag but to MOTIVATE! A healthy, active, vibrant life can be yours!

Whenever you start to doubt whether you have

time to exercise, ask yourself this question: Would I willingly play Russian roulette with my life? Of course not! Don't play Russian roulette with your health anymore. Good health is far better than any material possession or financial gain. You deserve the best of what life has to offer.

When it comes to your health you will be way ahead if you use something that is not very common, and that is common sense! Every day, as you look around you, see the signs of common sense not being used. The fast food drive-up windows are full of people who have ignored the common sense rule that fat taken in yields to fat staying in your body, especially when you don't do anything to combat the fat stores and weight increase. Cigarettes are not good for your health but millions of American still smoke. Yes, common sense ain't that common! That's why I mentioned the analogy of playing Russian roulette; many people I know are figuratively placing a gun to their head by constantly refusing to invest in their health. You suggest they go for a walk but they'd rather take a nap. You tell them to ease up on the salt and they sprinkle on more.

I may be 58 but I remember the days of my parents telling me not to do this or that and, not knowing any better, I rebelled. Now, as I look back, I realize they were right and were only looking out for my good. Today there is a plethora of commercials, bill boards, TV shows, and magazines telling us to exercise, cut fat intake, and increase the amount of fiber we consume. You might rebel by eating that donut, putting an extra slab of butter on that roll, or by postponing taking action toward a fitness regime. Your health is one area that you DON'T want to look back at and wish you would have heeded wise advice.

4 BALANCING YOUR HEALTH BUDGET
*Don't write a check with your body
that you can't afford to cash*

A balanced budget is important in any financial plan. When a company's financial records don't add up then there is a big problem. Perhaps, at one time, your personal financial records got out of balance. Remember what havoc that wreaked and how hard you worked to get things back into right order? Well, maybe you have been eating more calories than you can burn off in a day. Perhaps you are several pounds over-weight and have watched your diet and exercise closely for three whole days when the temptation to splurge at the office party arises. You justify this 'exception' and go ahead and fill your plate with goodies. You just cashed a check your body can't afford to pay. You have no reserve in your account so you just got yourself deeper in debt. Don't get frustrated—get determined to have a balanced health budget.

Budget Out Laziness

Laziness is insidious. It is sly and goes unnoticed. It hides behind your senseless excuses and can block your future success. Laziness seeks company! You've heard the saying, misery loves company. Well, lazy people tend to hang with lazy people. Laziness can be unforgiving if left unchecked. I knew a man who recently passed away from lung cancer, which according to his doctor was caused by smoking. His doctor had been telling him for years to stop smoking but he never listened. He had excuses like "it's too hard," "I can quit anytime I want to," and "I'll do it later." Laziness had won in this area of his life. It has been two years since he passed away and all that knew him are aware that his untimely death could have been prevented had he been proactive and applied action to his situation. He knew exactly what to do but did not activate his will power to take that action. It is the same with all of us when we know what to do but have failed to do it consistently. There are many diseases that can be prevented by eating healthy and exercising consistently. We just need to get off our lackadaisical rear ends and start to take action. I speak like I do because I want to see all people improve the quality of their lives. For in the same way that I have reaped the benefits of good health and a younger, stronger body, I want others to reap good health as well. Life is too short, my friend, to not live it in quality with more energy, and enthusiastically. This only comes from living a healthy life.

Assessing the Risk

There are many things about which you take risks, chances, and gambles regarding the choices for your lives and those of your family and loved ones. You make decisions not really knowing exactly what the results will be. Sometimes they turn out to be wise decisions, sometimes you simply learn a good lesson, and sometimes you discover that your decision has brought about devastating results. This is a part of life, right? But then there are times when you know for certain that a decision is for the very best and will bring wonderful, life-long, positive results. Those are the decisions you need to whole heartedly jump into! Being physically fit is near the top of the wisest decisions you can make in your entire life. Peak physical fitness pays out dividends that bring joy and happiness that no amount of money can buy. NOW is the time to make this choice for your life and the life of your family.

Starting a fitness program can produce a mix of thoughts and emotions. There is the exhilaration of doing something good for yourself that you have put off too long yet fear that you may not be strong enough to accomplish much. There is a gust of determination and yet concern that you may let it fall to the wayside like so many times before. Again, attitude is key in reaching your goal of physical health and fitness. To help form a great attitude toward fitness let's look at the risks of not making the decision for change today.

STRESS-The keys to great health are in exercise, nutrition, rest, meditation, and a life of reduced stress. That's right, a life of reduced stress. You notice I did not say a life without stress because as long as you are living there will be times when your stress buttons are pushed. How you handle the stress will depend upon actively using those keys mentioned above. Quite frequently, people will ask me how my day is going and I usually respond, "Great!" That is because I made a decision years ago to not allow what is happening in the moment to affect the rest of my day. For example, if my car broke down in the middle of a busy intersection and I was late for work, it would probably frustrate me a little but it would not mess up my day. If you do not control your emotions, your emotions will control you. I have had bad things happen in a day but I could not tell you when I had a bad day. First of all, I have too much to do and accomplish to let the normal things in life affect my entire day. This is important to understand because there will be times when you feel like you are too upset or too busy to exercise. These are the times when you will need to stay resolute and figure out when you are going to get in your workouts. Life is a learning experience! What you do with that experience can make and shape you. Look around you and you will see people choosing their paths in life. Some are choosing great health while others are striving for material wealth. These two do not have to be mutually exclusive. There are people who are well off financially and who do respect themselves enough to take care of their health. They are the smart ones who understand that they must pay themselves first physically. If you keep your body in good physical condition you are more equipped to not only meet your needs but also the needs and wants of many others. When your body is properly cared for the longer you will be able to provide service to your family, business, and community.

Stress is a powerful force over our lives. Jobs, family, bills, health, etc., can be a source of stress and frustration. Stress can have an impact on our attitude in and about life. We all experience it. Many develop poor eating habits such as over-eating. Some handle stress through alcohol and drug use, and some become depressed and isolated from others. This list could go on and on. These behaviors bring about the physical destitution of our bodies, taking years off our lives even while everything may be looking wonderfully prosperous to those on the outside looking in. These undisciplined lifestyles are headed toward an end that is not what one would plan for or desire. Careless living is inadvertently being planned for once the knowledge arrives! The truth is that to continue handling stress in this manner is a set-up for obesity, illness, and disease. We have all read that being under stress can lead to illnesses and it can often have an impact on one's attitude. Can you recall your attitude, disposition, or behavior changing when you've been under stress? Sometimes it happens without you even being aware that it is happening. You may have found yourself having negative feelings about a person or situation that you would not have had under other circumstances. Making the decision and taking the action to become physically fit, coupled with a healthy diet, are powerful weapons against stress and extraordinary tools for a healthy life.

DEPRESSION- When we are burdened down with stressful situations—like too many bills and not enough income—it affects us mentally and emotionally. Just think of those days that you made exercise a priority. Didn't you feel better throughout the day, knowing that you made that good choice of investing in your health? Now think about how you feel when you put off working out until the end of the day when you are too tired to get off of the couch. I have encountered many people who said that exercise and fitness training kept depression and other mood disorders at bay or lessened their negative effect. For more information on this subject go back and read Mental and Emotional Strength in Chapter Two.

LACK OF ENERGY-Lack of energy begets lack of energy. Have you ever noticed that when you are feeling tired and dragged out but you get out and exercise anyway you suddenly have more energy than when you started? On the flip-side, when you are experiencing low energy and opt for lounging around doing the minimal amount to get through your day you feel more tired and lethargic. Exercise increases your heart-rate which brings needed oxygen to cells, causes your respiratory rate to increase to provide the oxygen, and causes you to warm up; all these can leave you feeling invigorated. Also, increased muscle mass can increase your metabolism, which is another energy boost.

DISEASE-When people eat in an unhealthy manner they become increasingly over weight which is most often the beginning of serious health problems that could possibly lead to a shortened life span and many visits to the hospital along the way. No matter how smart you are, a great mind cannot operate out of a dead body. Isn't it easy to eat that donut, candy bar, soda, and fries throughout the day and not think about the consequences? It is so easy for people to allow themselves to be deceived into thinking that all is well in their bodies as they abuse them in this manner. They are continuing to rise each day, accomplish daily tasks, and enjoy life as if everything is alright. It's similar to spending all the money you take in each month. The months go by and it seems as if all is well. But then comes the unexpected emergency—and I mean a true emergency. You then realize that if you had only put a small amount away every month you could easily have overcome the situation.

That is what happens to your body when you don't put regular deposits in your health account. People choose to believe that all is well but the pounds are increasing, their body mass is becoming greater, their bodies are becoming weaker, and they consistently open themselves up for unexpected emergencies. These emergencies are in the form of obesity, heart disease, circulation problems, joint problems and others leading to a shortened and unpleasantly unhealthy life. Isn't it wonderful that we have the ability to change our attitudes and to take action? Isn't it wonderful to know that we have the power to plan for a future with the best possible health? Wouldn't it be sad to ignore such an opportunity? If I had a choice to become cash poor or to become physically poor, believe me, I'd choose to become cash poor. I can recover from that, I know for a fact. But becoming physically poor can lead to consequences that are not necessarily reversible.

Removing the Risk

So, now that you are aware of the risks of inaction, stop planning for obesity, illness, and disease. Instead, love yourself enough to overcome the negative responses to stress. Walking, running, working out, playing physical games, eating a healthy diet, etc., are your weapons for combating the stresses in life. Let them replace improper eating habits, wine, beer, alcohol, drugs, mood swings, depression, or whatever negative behavior is currently being used to combat stressful situations.

Becoming physically fit truly takes a conscious mental attitude to make it happen. NOW is the time. It is as simple as eating in moderation and exercising regularly. Moderation practiced in all that we think and do would make for a great life. As it pertains to our bodies, we would not be overeating or selecting the wrong foods. We wouldn't have two sizes of clothing (or more!) for our bigger and smaller selves. This type of moderation would mean having more energy, being able to move around more easily, and not being as tired. Moderation is being balanced. We monitor our check book so we have the proper balance; we monitor our health by having annual physicals; we go to the dentist twice a year to monitor our dental condition; and we have annual reviews on our jobs to be sure our performance is achieving or exceeding expectations. It is time to monitor our physical fitness and eating habits. When was the last time you were physically fit? Come on, when was it? Have you been there in the past, or have you never been physically fit? When was the last time you implemented healthy eating habits? NOW is the time. You can do this. You really can! How? *With moderation and commitment.*

Health Assets

Consider what you have been given. Each of us has the gift of a wonderfully constructed body for which we are personally responsible. God created our bodies as a vehicle in which reside both our spirit and our soul. Having been given this amazing body we are responsible for keeping it, along with our mind and spirit, fit for their intended purposes. Although this is our responsibility, we do have a choice in the matter. We daily choose to carefully care for our body and its components or to ignore what is required for its intended purpose. We make those choices by making and maintaining habits that are repeated millions of times during the course of our lives. Some of those choices are very good. For many, however, far too many of the choices are very poor. The trouble with habitually doing negative things to one's body over one's life is that it results in the abuse of this precious gift and the probable consequence of its early destruction.

Perhaps you've never looked at your body as an entrusted gift before. Perhaps you have merely gone thus far in life taking your body for granted, expecting it to provide for you the great function you expect and desire. Or, perhaps you are well aware of the need to better care for your body but have been hiding from the fact that you need to make some changes. Often times in life you need a little helping hand, someone who is more knowledgeable in the area of physical fitness, someone who can provide guidance, share their wisdom/expertise, caringly hold you accountable as you reach your goals, and who has done it themselves and won't judge you for just getting started! It stands to reason that everyone (well, at least most everyone) would prefer to have a strong body and a strong mind. So, what stands in the way? I could list page after page of reasons. The bottom line is that most don't seek help in the attainment of becoming healthy, fit, and strong. Why is help needed? Because we get so caught up in the affairs of life we do not take the time that is needed to get our bodies where we need to be.

Benefits of a Personal Trainer

Would you sincerely like to make a lifelong change that will make you proud to look in the mirror (as opposed to hiding from it), feel young and strong, enjoy greater health, and become physically fit? A personal trainer can help you set, reach and maintain goals that are appropriate for you and will guide you to those benefits. At this point you may be saying, "Okay, Ron, I understand that it is necessary to take better care of myself and that it is up to me to do something about it, but I can do this on my own." My response, generally, is that it's a great statement! However, why haven't you done it? Have you tried? Have you tried and failed by getting started and then stopping? It can be hard to get motivated and then to stay motivated on your own. Additionally, you really don't have the knowledge that a personal trainer brings into your life. Let me put it this way: When suffering from a horrific tooth ache you visit the dentist for relief. If a loved one is suffering from severe depression you help them get psychological or medical assistance. If your child is struggling in math we expect the teacher to provide tools necessary to get the concepts across. When you undertake a new career or business venture you look to the experts, those who have already successfully done what you desire to do, for knowledge and guidance. Why should it be any different when it comes to becoming physically fit, especially when we consider the overall benefits?

There are many things to consider when making the decision to work with a personal trainer. Watching a video can demonstrate how to do various exercises but it cannot observe you to be sure you are doing them correctly. Improper appropriation can bring about, at the least, little to no effect, and at the most, serious injury--neither of which you want. A fitness trainer makes sure that every movement is safe, accurately focused on a specific set of muscles, and is optimized for the greatest possible benefit. A fitness trainer is totally focused on your body condition and requirements, planning the exercises specifically designed according to your needs and goals. A fitness trainer will consider your age and current level of fitness and develop a program that is appropriately paced. From there the level of intensity will grow as you develop the strength and stamina along the way. It is amazingly rewarding! So even if you think you are too old, too physically unfit, too injury prone or too unmotivated, recognize that these are great reasons to have a fitness trainer. The expertise helps you develop the discipline that one-on-one training brings by keeping you accountable. You will see benefits you never knew were possible. NOW IS THE TIME!

After having made the decision to work with a personal trainer it is necessary to select that professional with caution. Just like you use wisdom in making a decision about an attorney, tax consultant, or physician, you want to be certain that the personal trainer you select has qualities that merit your involvement. After all, it's your body we are talking about in addition to your investment of time and finances. Having worked with hundreds of clients over three decades of one-on-one personal training sessions, there are some insights I would like to share with you regarding making the right selection. Ask the prospective trainer questions which will help you evaluate where he or she stands in these areas. When seeking recommendations from others, be sure to ask them these types of questions as well.

1. Does the trainer care more about YOU than making money? Would you be just another paycheck or is the trainer sincerely interested in your success?

2. Does the trainer take the time to know you, your habits, condition, and goals? Is there rapport between the two of you? Do you sense a dedication to your success? Are you truly important?

3. Does the trainer demonstrate a strong body? Does the trainer actually practice what he or she preaches and is personally successful in what is being taught to others? This will help you have confidence that what is being promoted can really work. It also shows self-discipline and gives the trainer the right to correct and motivate you, the client, in what has to take place to be successful.

4. Does the trainer totally focus attention on the clients every move, consistently correcting the slightest improper movement and positioning? Is his/her attention divided between other activities or thoughts or are you the only important activity in the room?

5. Does the trainer use caution in giving recommendations for your exercise program to be sure that only the best is recommended for you? Is it customized for your needs, while making necessary adjustments as required? Does the trainer ask you for feedback as to how you are feeling, what you are experiencing, and what you can handle?

6. Is the trainer honest in his/her dealings and

truthful in communicating?

7. Does the trainer hold you accountable to fully participate in the program, giving it your all during every moment? Does the trainer encourage you to do additional activities between sessions and hold you accountable?

You are probably aware that many health clubs hire individuals to work as personal trainers. Their clientele come to the club, and rather than going through the gym on their own, they do so with the trainer. This is amongst all of the intensity and noise level that goes along with being in the health club filled with others working out. After that comment you may think I'm a little biased. Well, you're right! Of course, it is possible to find a good trainer who is dedicated to the clientele. As regular club employees, you may find that the motivation to see success in each client is lacking. Think about it. Their salary is typically not based on how well the client is doing.

Over the years I have found that the better trainers seek to work on their own independently from a health club. It's also interesting to note that motivation is at a much higher level when the trainer is self-employed. The only way to keep clients coming back is to help them achieve positive results. That in itself is motivation. As business owners they know the importance of reputation and positive 'word of mouth' marketing. Hence, there is an internal mechanism that helps stimulate the proper motivation needed to help clients become physically fit. Additionally, working privately with a personal trainer gives you privacy and the ability for you and your trainer to focus on you and you alone! It's all about you, you know! Ask as many people as you can for recommendations of a personal trainer. The person you want should have a track record of excellence and an outstanding reputation.

Clients should be able to testify of the trainer's sincere devotion to their success and of an outstanding relationship with the trainer which continues to develop over the months and often times years, if so desired.

Whether you decide to work with an independent, self-employed trainer or one who works inside a health club, be careful in your selection. Keep in mind that a younger trainer may not have the experience that a seasoned trainer will have. Yes, it's important for everyone to get a start in their career, but this is an area where you may want to work with someone who has a trained eye which comes only from experience. It has taken many years to get to the point when, instinctively, I can determine how and what needs to be done to avoid client frustration, over exertion, and potential injury. In my opinion, an experienced, seasoned trainer is the best of all choices, as long as they also meet the criteria previously discussed.

I must again emphasize that upon selecting a personal trainer you must seek direction from your physician. It is important to then share with your trainer any restrictions that need to be placed on your new exercise program. You will also discuss with your trainer any prior injuries as well as limitations. You will answer questions about your lifestyle, eating habits, smoking and drinking habits, current exercising practices, exercise programs in which you have previously participated as well as other questions. You will also discuss your personal goals such as your desired weight, appearance, strength and stamina, and the possible barriers that need to be overcome. All of this information will be important as your trainer puts together a program tailored for the attainment of your goals. You will then begin your program with focused results. You will start out slowly and then gradually increase your routines. You will begin to notice muscles where there were previously none, stamina you haven't felt for a long time and strength to do things that once seemed impossible. These are the benefits of the attitude and action discussed in the previous chapter. It's amazing what we can accomplish when we put our mind and effort to the matter. Remember how we repetitively do things to our bodies on a daily, yearly, and decade basis. Now is the time to make the change and receive the benefits you long for and deserve. Yes, I said deserve!

So what kind of a commitment is needed in order to achieve the benefit of a stronger and healthier body? I recommend a minimum of three to four workout sessions each week combining weight bearing exercises with some form of aerobic activity. This consistency will build a lifetime habit for ongoing fitness.

No Quick Fix

You have probably noticed all of the hype in recent years about anti-aging this and anti-aging that. Millions of dollars are being spent yearly on our desire to appear younger than we are and to keep it that way forever! The purchase of cosmetics (nothing new there!), face lifts and other cosmetic surgeries, hair replacements, body enhancements, liposuction, dental implants, vein removers, tummy tucks, hormone replacements—the list goes on and on—is at an all-time high. Most of us want to look younger than our age (while the very young want to look older, of course). Many will do whatever it takes to keep from looking our actual age. The latest new discovery to the fountain of youth is never-ending and is always being purchased. There is such an emphasis on our outer appearance which adds no longevity to our lives!

There is nothing wrong with wanting to look good and taking measures to enhance our natural beauty. It can make life more enjoyable for ourselves and for others who look at us! There was an old television advertisement that said something like *when you look good you feel good and when you feel good you do good.* Makes sense to me! But quite honestly, it becomes tremendously shallow when compared to spending those efforts on activities that not only make us look better (being fit does this) but also brings about greater health, fitness, bodily and mental strength, endurance, better mood, and often a greater joy of life. Shouldn't those things be our foremost quest followed by the rest? Somehow we seem to have gotten things twisted. We eat what we want, spend what's necessary for temporary beauty, and then rest in our favorite place as couch potatoes! On the flip side, we could be walking the dog, eating healthy, going to training, and enjoying the health our bodies deserve and the sharp mind with which we were born. Investing in your body should come first, even before investing in a bank account. Pay yourself with fitness training first! Make it a priority. Then when you pay yourself from your finances (secondarily) your health will allow you to more greatly (and gratefully) enjoy your finances. It is a concept too powerful to ignore. Take a moment and think about it.

One of the biggest benefits I have observed my clients achieve is a slowed down aging process. Becoming physically fit is a way by which we can not only look better but we can also cause the aging process to be slowed. Who wouldn't want that to happen? That simple and powerful fact should help motivate you to do something about where you currently are! Many of my clients have come to me looking much older than their years, then after consistent training, look much younger than they did when they first arrived. It is truly amazing to see. Being overweight, out of shape, and without strength and vitality all aid in adding years to one's appearance. Don't you want to live each year with energy, looking and feeling like you are at your prime, no matter your age? It happens to those who get and stay fit. There is no reason why you cannot attain that status. I have often taken a picture of clients when they get started. After several months of consistent training I take another picture. They are always astonished at their improvement. It reminds me of a flower that starts out small then slowly, gradually, blooms into a beautiful specimen. It happens so slowly that you really don't notice it as it is happening but then, there it is in all of its radiance. That's why I take the pictures. It's hard for the client to see the changes as they are taking place but over time those gradual changes are occurring. What joy it brings to see amazement on the faces of those who have changed their attitude and changed their actions after recognizing the benefit of doing so. Remember, once you have the knowledge you are then responsible for putting it to use. You no longer have the excuse of "I didn't know." I am sharing with you facts and actual experiences. It can happen for you, also, if you let it! I trust that you will take the steps to slow down the aging process.

There is yet another benefit I have come to observe over my years of training others. Care to take a guess? You've got it: Becoming physically fit means you also gain a greater resistance to illness. That can't be new news, but it certainly is news that is neglected by most people! Allow me to use one of my clients in demonstrating how physical fitness fights off health issues. The premier sports anchor in the state of Minnesota is Mark Rosen of the local CBS affiliate WCCO. When Mark began training with me over nineteen years ago he was always getting sick. About every third to fourth week he was catching a cold, etc. On top of that, it would take a very long time for him to recover from those various bouts. I don't know about you, but feeling sick can seem to affect so many areas of life from job, to energy levels, to emotional wellness. When it is happening repeatedly, that can really be a downer. I am happy to report that Mark continued coming to his training classes, which has ultimately resulted in him not only becoming physically fit but his health has greatly improved as well. Now, whenever he does get sick it does not last nearly as long as in the past. Mark loves having a greatly improved immune system, feeling fantastic almost all of the time, having a high energy level, plus looking good! Way to go, Mark Rosen!

Mark had the desire and tenacity to make necessary changes in his life. He saw an opportunity and took advantage of it. How often do you and I have examples all around us, which if taken seriously, can make a 'forever difference' in our lives? We need to slow down a bit and notice what may seem like a small thing and determine how it can be applied to our overall life. I can think of an occasion as a youngster which had a life-long impact. As a little boy I remember waking up early in the morning to see Jack LaLanne on television. Year after year I'd watch him do push-ups, pull ups, jumping jacks—all those things that became his trademarks. Although I never met him personally, he became one of my original mentors, motivating me to become what he was—a real fitness motivator! In 2009 I had the opportunity of a lifetime to interview Jack LaLanne on a local radio show that I was co-hosting with Mark Rosen. I give Jack the credit for making that 'forever difference' in my life. Jack dedicated his life to encouraging people to better themselves through exercise and fitness. He is one who has always lived what he preached. I had to mention him in this book because he set so many great examples of what it means to be physically independent. It was a life-long journey for him; even in his nineties he looked more like seventy, and yes, he was financially fit as well! Jack passed away almost one year after our interview, but his influence over my life and the lives of others will never be forgotten. If you could only have one--physical or financial health--which would you choose?

While writing in a coffee shop one cold Minnesota morning, I came to know someone else who had made a 'forever difference' in the lives of those around her. As a fit and healthy looking woman passed me with a cup of coffee I couldn't help but ask her what she does to stay in such great shape. I was very impressed when she said she runs and lifts weights. She could tell I was impressed and when asked how long she had been doing this, she said twenty years! She was forty-eight and looked much younger. I asked if she got her good habits from her parents but she said "no" and that, although her father is financially well off, his health is very poor. "That's why my daughter and granddaughter exercise," she said. This fit lady from Sweden turned the tide for her family and made what is sure to be a 'forever difference' in their lives. Before she left the coffee shop I just had to ask how working out made her feel? "I'm so happy to have this influence on my daughter's life and others around me," she responded. "I have peace and feel mentally and socially alive!" Powerful, I thought. We can take a given situation, like what she saw her father experience, and either follow in his footsteps or turn it into something positive. Also, others can watch us do something positive and turn it into a monumental experience in their lives. What power we have! Let's try to see what things we can give to and receive from others who are around us each and every day. Let's learn from and give away those 'forever differences.'

Becoming Financially and Physically Fit

Consider what things families who are financially well-off typically do to attain and maintain that status. They usually:

1. Pay themselves first because they value themselves.

2. Make smart investments because they value their futures.

3. Automate direct deposits because it becomes less painful that way!

4. Make financial commitments and stick to them.

Since we would like to master our money so that it does not end up mastering us, I'm sure we will agree that these four simple yet vital steps are do-able. We just have to put forth the conscious effort to make it happen. If we do, it can result in a very positive and significant impact upon our lives and futures. The lady from Sweden probably saw her father implement these patterns into their family's lifestyle resulting in her ability to discuss with me his financial success. Sadly, he did not put the same standards into his physical being which has resulted in his poor health. What if he had applied the principles he used in finance to his health? Would you suppose he would be better equipped to enjoy his wealth and his family?

Unifying Your Family Through Exercise

Regular exercise can help to bring your family closer together. You have probably heard the saying a house divided against itself can't stand. That is because when there is constant conflict between spouses or family members a wedge is driven in and this causes separation. That wedge can come in earlier in life than expected due to physical health problems due to neglect. Instead of enjoying each other's company, one spouse is spending their time taking care of the other much earlier than what they could have imagined. But a family that exercises together grows old together! When one spouse does not take care of themselves, this neglect could bring unwanted heartache to the family, creating a division between the healthy and the unhealthy, the ones that care and the ones that don't. Sometimes jealousy will come into the marriage when one spouse feels threaten by the other one's younger and healthier appearance or new found energy. Think about it! Every day we encounter people who look and act older than they actually are. In most cases this has come from lack of exercise and just plain old bad eating habits. State fairs and conventions are all great places to do some people watching. The wear and tear on an old person's back due to the fact that they were carrying too much weight in their mid-section has caused the person to slump. In many cases this could have been prevented if they had been on a consistent exercise program.

Health Bank Account

If you are like many people, you most likely do whatever you can to financially provide for your daily needs and desires. You work hard to accomplish your dreams whether large or small. You put years into paying for college, a car, a home, or great vacations. You work long hours to acquire those extra things that make life more enjoyable. You may even work tirelessly to be able to have the type of retirement fund from which a comfortable life can be enjoyed in your 'golden years.' Admirable! Fantastic! Wise! Let me ask, however, just how admirable, fantastic, and wise is it to make all of these awesome deposits into one's financial account but make no or very few deposits into one's health account? Remember, it does no good to have wealth and not be able to enjoy what that wealth can afford because you neglected to make the corresponding deposits toward your greatest asset--your health.

The first time you opened up a bank account it was probably with small deposits. At times it may have been painful to make those deposits, especially if you were in the habit of undisciplined spending or if income was tight. In time those regular deposits grew as you grew in discipline and earnings. There is nothing wrong with small deposits. They help you keep consistency in your commitment and bring about an increase in positive attitudes about saving money. When making deposits becomes a habit there is a sense of accomplishment as you watch your bank account grow. It may have been painful at first but you committed to taking those steps according to your supply.

The same is true when you open your health account. Start off playing it smart by making small but consistent deposits. This will help you to avoid injuries, physical strain, and negative thoughts about continuing. It is very important to keep a positive attitude about your exercise commitment and to work out a minimum of three times per week. When you start getting into better shape you can increase the intensity and scope of your fitness program. A positive attitude, commitment, and consistency over time are the necessary deposits into your health account that can lead to more energy to accomplish your goals and reserve to enjoy the process.

Making Deposits

I'm guessing you weren't born yesterday, right? That being the case, you've had any given number of years to develop some not-so-good habits. It just seems to go with the territory of being human beings. Those habits often result in becoming obstacles that hold us back from being successful in keeping our promises, reaching our goals, and other various aspects of life. The good news is that once you are more consciously aware of obstacles (harmful habits) you can face and overcome them. You have identified what you are going to do (in the last chapter). With this vision and commitment in the forefront of your mind, you can develop your new lifestyle of physical fitness. Make the decision to do this with a 'can do' attitude and a determination to tackle every obstacle that would try to keep you where you were yesterday. Your today is a brand new day! Now, let's take a look at three of those obstacles: food, time and money.

Food Intake

One common obstacle to becoming physically fit is our food intake, both what we eat and how much we eat. Yes, what you have heard is true; exercise works hand in hand with what and how much you put in your mouth. Exercise will help reduce the waistline but it will take a life changing, new habit to keep it trim. If your intake has been an obstacle you are among the majority. But starving yourself is not the answer. Going on the latest trendy diet usually is not the answer. So, what new eating habits should you focus on developing? It's a matter of changing the way you eat forever. Otherwise, if you decide to go on a diet and then get off the diet once you've lost weight, guess what typically happens? Oh, you know already? So making a life-long change is the answer. Does that mean you will never be able to have a piece of cake or glass of punch again? No, that is not realistic. But to do so on occasion, once you've reached your goals, is part of the fun of living.

First, let's focus on what to eat:

- EAT lots of colorful vegetables and salads

(minus the butter, oils, and fatty/sweet dressings!) The internet has fantastic dressings you can make that are oil and sugar free.

- EAT fresh fruit (minus the juices!)

- EAT small portions of fish, poultry, and occasionally red meat (bake it, broil it, grill it, but don't fry it!)

- EAT brown: rice, pasta, whole wheat bread (minimum)

- EAT sweet potatoes/yams instead of white potatoes

Don'ts:

- Sweets / Soda / Fruit juice / Sugar

- Snack foods, fast foods

- White bread, rice, potatoes

- Fried foods

- Packaged foods

- Processed foods

Small Portions Only:

- Nuts

- Beans

The above list is not all-inclusive but what I have

found to be of great help over the years. Also, whenever possible, buy organic products! And, if you have a juicer, use it to juice your vegetable—as much as you want!

Another way to overcome the obstacle of food as you move toward becoming physically fit is to set an example. Many of us feel responsible for the well-being of others and that can be used to a great advantage. For instance, as an adult, become determined to be an example for those around you, whether they are children, grandchildren, nieces, nephews, spouse, parents, friends, or co-workers. Realize that you can make a difference in their lives as you change your eating habits.

Time Investment

Don't allow time to pass you by! Seize the moment, smell the roses, bike, walk, jog, swim, exercise your mind as well as your body. In any given day, how much time are you spending doing literally nothing (which, by the way, is good to do sometimes)? Our bodies, just like our cars, do need to rest in order to run efficiently. But how much time are we spending even in our bathrooms reading the same old magazines? Ten minutes? Twenty? Perhaps even thirty minutes, while all along time is passing us by.

There is no better time in your life than RIGHT NOW! Yes, right now! Make a decision to exercise and then to stick with that decision. You are either seizing your time or allowing time to seize you. Allow me to give you an example: A friend of mine for years has talked about starting an exercise program. Year after year I have been listening to him spout off about how he needs to lose weight and how diabetes runs in his family and so on. It has been over ten years since the first time he began to talk about starting an exercise program, but to this date he has not made a real commitment to exercise. Time has seized him. He has been so busy building his business, buying his cars, and taking his dream vacations, while all along neglecting his health. He has amassed wealth but time has seized his health. You can have both but you must have commitment to your health as a priority.

Money

Another common obstacle that tries to block your physical fitness success is finances. You may wonder, "Where is the money coming from to add a personal trainer and any other expenses for this fitness lifestyle?" It's a good question that needs a real answer. Just like extra physical weight causes strain to the body, extra spending can cause strain to your checking account. If this is an obstacle due to the need of better money management, and it normally is, there are ways to overcome. In doing so, you will be able to re-prioritize your spending and make the health investment you need in order to pay yourself first physically. It has been said that the more we make, the more we spend. I tend to believe that. It is so easy to spend it all but there were times when we did not have that much to spend! There is always something to buy. You've got to search out those areas that can be disposed of and replace them with investing in your health and fitness. Here are some things to consider:

- Write and implement a budget and adhere to it consistently.

- Reduce, (better yet, remove) all unhealthy expenditures, i.e., mochas, sodas, fast-food, sweets, snacks.

- Prepare a lunch from home instead of eating out.

- Cut out bad habits like smoking, stopping after work for a drink, etc.

- Cut back on such things as cable TV.

- Get a less-expensive cell phone plan.

- Car pool more frequently.

- Consolidate errands to use less gas.

Each household is unique in its spending. If you take a real close look you will find additional ways in which you can develop your family fitness budget. Following that budget will result in a lifestyle of health that can forever change your life and the lives of those around you. You will be amazed at what YOU can do for YOU. You have an opportunity to invest in your today and your future. Don't let a cable bill or daily lunches be the obstacle that stands in your way. Overcome it and put your money where you deserve for it to go. You will thank yourself down the road, I promise you! What you spend now on your fitness can save you tens of thousands of dollars and tremendous heart ache due to health issues that physical fitness can help avoid. So what is important? Where are the misplaced priorities? It's time to make a change.

5 RE-FIRE-MENT PLAN
Whatever you would give to get your health back, give now to keep it!

You may know people who in the prime of their life had great financial strength. Having worked hard for years to attain the good life, they suddenly find themselves with an illness that is often avoidable such as diabetes, stroke, or heart attack just to name a few. Their health outcome was one which could have been avoided with proper diet and exercise but made excuses and didn't develop the mental attitude or apply the needed physical action. It is a story we hear from friends and neighbors every day and it is very sad. It is true that proper diet and exercise does not prevent all infirmities but the odds are greatly reduced. You are worth doing everything you can to achieve and maintain good health. It would be horrible to be laying in a hospital bed, overhearing the medical staff commenting among themselves, "What a shame it is that he didn't take good care of himself. It didn't have to turn out this way had he just taken the right actions." Obviously, you would gladly trade the money you had accumulated for the opportunity to enjoy good health. You would also gladly balance your priorities so this would not be your story. Plan to live a long, healthy, and prosperous life by taking action. Begin making the physical deposits into your health account NOW and grow that account daily! Having your health, well, it's worth everything.

ReFIREment, Not ReTIREment!

The days of retiring at age forty or fifty are long gone. People are finding they have to work longer just to pay their mortgage. The American Dream might be threatened by our economy but your health does not have to suffer because of it. Healthy longevity can only happen if you have realized your physical dream and kept yourself in good health. As a teenager I can remember seeing in the back of magazines like popular mechanics, pictures of men who were fit or men who went from scrawny to muscular because they lifted weights. Even if the American dream has put a damper on your finances it does not have to put a damper on your health. Any man or women can make a change for the good—physically or mentally—if they desire. The real question is: Do you believe enough in yourself to make exercise a priority in your life? Do you love yourself enough to start eating like you know you should? If you do, then you have all that is necessary to begin making these changes. Throw out the excuses and reap the benefits of a healthier life.

If you ask most people if they have any health benefits they would immediately think of what type of health plan and what the medical insurance covers. When I speak of benefits I speak of something that never runs out until we leave this earth. It is a Better Life benefit—exercise and healthy eating keeps your body and mind more tuned and keeps you out of the doctor's office or nursing home! The quality of your life is dependent on what you have done or what you do from this point onward.

Maybe you're saying that at your age it won't make

a difference—you're either a young adult who is fit and trim or a senior citizen. To that I ask, "How do you know it won't make a difference?" If you have never committed to starting and sticking to an exercise regimen, I can tell you that at any age you will improve. You will have more energy. You will feel stronger. Whatever it does, it will be an improvement over where you are now. You may not be overweight and may be able to do your daily routine activities now, but a body that is left to itself will eventually find itself in trouble. Doctors call this "deconditioning". The less you do physically the weaker you become and the less agile you are. Seniors who walk and exercise are less likely to need (or postpone the need for) assistive devices such as canes and walkers. They are also less likely to have balance problems which increases the incidence of falls and the plight of senior citizens—a broken hip. Exercise is one of the single biggest factors contributing to your health so don't let your youth fool you! If you don't take care to preserve and strengthen what you have while you can, you will eventually wish you did.

Perhaps you just don't like to exercise. Well, if exercise is not enjoyable, my friend, find something that you can do on a regular basis that will burn the calories. If you don't like walking then find ways to spice it up. Get some headphones and listen to motivation messages or some inspiring and motivating music. Use that time walking to meditate or to enjoy nature. There is something out there for everybody. You just need to find what works for you. Don't try to be like Joe down the street. Be who you are right now but do something! While you're at it, stop saying you don't like exercise. Start speaking what you wish was true; that you do like exercise and that you love how you feel when you get back from a long walk. Make sure your exercise program is fun and something you enjoy doing.

Excuses never helped anyone achieve any worthwhile endeavor. Remember, you are better than your excuses. Take the initiative and when you finish reading this book and are ready to begin exercising, take these points into consideration:

1. Is this form of exercise something I can do consistently?

2. Is it easy?

3. Is it convenient?

When it comes to starting and staying on an exercise program, it is far better to build consistency versus an occasional hard work-out that only lasts for a few weeks, never to be visited again.

Sustained Vitality

Television sports anchorman, Mark Rosen, is an example of someone who takes investing in one's physical fitness seriously. He has kept the stamina and vitality necessary to maintain a successful career in the demanding field of television broadcasting. He knows the importance of paying yourself first physically. He writes:

> One of my favorite lines Hall of Fame coach, Bud Grant, used to say when he was with the Vikings was, "Durability is more important than ability." It took me a while but eventually it sunk in. He was right. As a head football coach you wanted to know which guys would play through the aches and pains and suit up for you on Sunday afternoon. You could have all the ability in the world, but if you spent your weeks in the whirlpool instead of the

practice field, you aren't much good to the coach. The same goes for the workplace. All of us know someone who, at the very first sniffle, is grabbing the phone to "call in sick".

I have accepted long hours as part of my weekly routine. I am often up at 7 a.m., driving to KFAN Radio for my 8 to 9 a.m. hour, then often doing another radio show with Gopher football coach Jerry Kill or recording a Viking's program before settling in to work another radio program in the afternoon. That does not even touch the time I spend writing and anchoring television sportscasts and covering other events for WCCO television. Most nights I don't end up heading for home until 11 p.m.

My twice weekly workouts with *The Fitness King* have enabled me to remain durable. I had just one sick day all year. We have to mentally take charge each day with an optimistic attitude to be at our best. I am now 61 years old but feel my overall health has allowed me to stay relevant in the ever changing news business and my associations with younger co-workers and adult kids.

There is no reason why any of us should act our age. I've never been this strong or feel more confident. Between the ears I am still 35 years old and just warming up! It's a glorious time to be alive. Why waste it? Get up off the couch, stay active, and move!

Mark Rosen is reaping the rewards of a balanced health account. He feels he is in the prime of life and is fit enough to take advantage of the opportunities that come his way. He is not sitting on his couch waiting for retirement so he can nurse his aches and pains. He is seizing life and enjoying it to the fullest.

Aging Gracefully

Today become resolute in your mind and then let it flow through to your body. Once it takes a hold of you, do what you know you should be doing. Do what the doctors have told you to do. Do what your spouse has suggested you do! Do what children have been praying that you would do. Start walking, start walking, start walking! Start walking slowly and then as you feel your body start to respond, pick up the pace. If you want to grow old gracefully you will have to move your body. Your body was designed for movement--to bend, to reach, to stretch. As you get up and start moving your body you will find yourself having more energy, feeling better, and sleeping better.

There are so many books out on the market that deal with health that I don't even want to go down that road. The road I want to go down is the one which I have seen with my own eyes; as a personal trainer with over 33 years of experience I breathe and I sleep good health. I have seen men and women from age forty to middle eighties add vigor to their lives and pep to their step. In fact, I recently spoke at a health and wellness conference and afterward a mature looking man name Francis approached me. He asked me how old I thought he looked. I thought for a second and I guessed his age to be sixty. He smiled and said, "I'm eighty-five years old!" I smiled back at him and said, "Now, that's what I'm talking about!" Here was man in his middle eighties looking sixty. Growing old with grace can be for everyone if we take what we have and move what we can. You too can grow old gracefully if you take out a little time each day and move your body.

Over 65 and Feeling Fit

As I mentioned earlier, I remember as a child being glued to our black and white TV watching the late Jack LaLanne go through his jumping jacks, his mountain climbers, and stomach crunches. All I could think was, "Wow! This man is in great shape. I want to be like him." As I got older, I would still see Jack on TV swimming in the ocean pulling boats and he was well into his late sixties at that time. Yes, Jack was a reminder to all of us of what CONSISTENT exercise could do for all of us regardless of our age. Over 65 and feeling fit is a life that all who desire can embrace and improve upon. When I interviewed Jack LaLanne he was ninety-two years of age and full of energy. He was still exercising on a daily basis. Jack contributed his great health to exercise and healthy eating. His motto was, "Exercise is King and nutrition is Queen. Put them together and you have a kingdom." I agree. His wife Elaine LaLanne has also stayed physically active and is a motivator for anyone who thinks that they're too old to change. Some of you remember witnessing the great actor, Jack Palance, dropping down and doing one-armed push-ups during the Academy Awards at the age of seventy-three. Jack LaLanne and Jack Palace are two men that were both in great shape well into their later years of life. Sixty-five can be the new fifty if you take action now.

Stay active. Stay excited. Stay moving. Remember, energy begets more energy. Don't let circumstances, your age, finances, or time constraints keep you from being active every single day. Don't stop moving until your last breath. Use every moment as an opportunity to take those steps and to keep building your health and fitness portfolio.

ENDING ENCOURAGEMENT QUESTIONNAIRE

1. Has your desire to get into shape increased from reading this book? _____

2. If your answer was yes, list the reasons below in the order of their importance. If your answer was no, re-read this book!

a. _____

b. _____

c. _____

d. _____

3. What do you feel exercise can do for you now?

a. _____

b. _____

c. _____

4. What are you going to do to make these changes that you desire?

_____

_____

_____

_____

4. When do you plan to take the actions necessary to affect this change? _____

I hope that this book has encouraged you to take the steps necessary to move you on your way to a healthy and productive life, for you, my friend, are worth it!

ABOUT THE AUTHOR

Ron Henderson, "The Fitness King," began his pursuit of personal fitness training over three decades ago. Ron is the author of *What is it Worth for You to Become Physically Fit* and *Fitness Economics.* He was notably the first personal fitness trainer in the Minneapolis/ St. Paul area to work with clients in their homes.

The success of his revolutionary approach is credited for Henderson's popularity as a media personality, spokesperson, and corporate trainer. Ron captivates and encourages audiences young and old alike, while educating, motivating, and inspiring them to enjoy more active lifestyles. He has trained top lawyers, hospital Chiefs of Staff, NFL players, and national recording stars and has helped them all to achieve physical fitness beyond what they could have done themselves.

Ron is the host of the *Fitness and Faith* exercise series, *The King and the Kids* workout show, and motivational series, *Motivation.* He also co-hosted *Fan Fitness Sundays* on KFAN radio with local celebrity Mark Rosen. Ron has been featured regularly in newspapers and magazines for over three decades.

In a 2007 radio interview, Elaine LaLanne, the wife of now deceased Jack LaLanne, remarked that Ron reminds her of a young Jack LaLanne with his passion and enthusiasm to inspire and motivate others. In 2009 the Minneapolis/St. Paul Business Journal awarded Ron the celebrated Minority Business Award.

www.ingramcontent.com/pod-product-compliance
Lightning Source LLC
Chambersburg PA
CBHW070901280326
41934CB00008B/1541